MAR 2017

Jump!

The Sound of J

By Cynthia Amoroso and Bob Noyed

2

I just jump in the lake.

I just jump with my brother Jake.

I just jump down the street.

I just jump
on my feet.

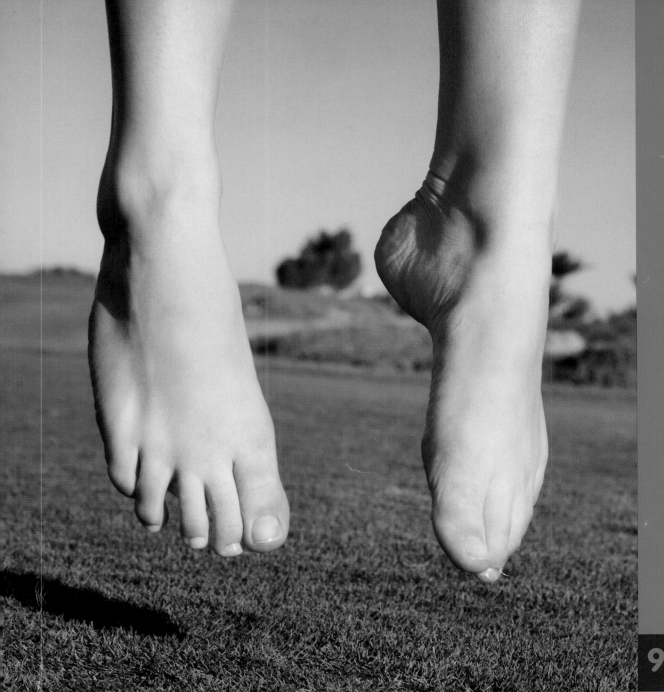

9

I just jump up so high.

11

I just jump
to reach
the sky.

13

14

I just jump
in the sand.

I just jump
on the land.

I just jump
and sing
a song.

19

I just jump all day long.

Word List:

jump

just

22

Note to Parents and Educators

The books in this series are based on current research, which supports the idea that our brains are pattern-detectors rather than rules-appliers. This means children learn to read easier when they are taught the familiar spelling patterns found in English. As children encounter more complex words, they have greater success in figuring out these words by using the spelling patterns.

Throughout the series, the texts provide the reader with the opportunity to practice and apply knowledge of the sounds in natural language. The books introduce sounds using familiar onsets and *rimes*, or spelling patterns, for reinforcement.

For example, the word *cat* might be used to present the short "a" sound, with the letter *c* being the onset and "_at" being the rime. This approach provides practice and reinforcement of the short "a" sound, as there are many familiar words made with the "_at" rime.

The stories and accompanying photographs in this series are based on time-honored concepts in children's literature: well-written, engaging texts and colorful, high-quality photographs combine to produce books that children want to read again and again.

Dr. Peg Ballard
Minnesota State University, Mankato

The Child's World®
childsworld.com

Published by The Child's World®
1980 Lookout Drive • Mankato, MN 56003-1705
800-599-READ • www.childsworld.com

ACKNOWLEDGMENTS
The Child's World®: Mary Swensen, Publishing Director
The Design Lab: Design
Michael Miller: Editing

PHOTO CREDITS
© Blend Images/Shutterstock.com: 14; Cameramannz/
Shutterstock.com: 17; karelnoppe/Shutterstock.com: 5;
Maxim Blinkov/Shutterstock.com: 10; MidoSemsem/
Shutterstock.com: 13; Monkey Business Images/
Shutterstock.com: cover, 2, 21; Pressmaster/Shutterstock.
com: 6; Sergey Novikov/Shutterstock.com: 18; Sergey
Peterman/Shutterstock.com: 9

ISBN 9781503809178
LCCN 2015958487

Printed in the United States of America
Mankato, MN
June, 2016
PA02310

ABOUT THE AUTHORS

Cynthia Amoroso holds undergraduate degrees in English and elementary education, and graduate degrees in curriculum and instruction as well as educational administration. She is currently an assistant superintendent in a suburban metropolitan school district. Cynthia's past roles include teacher, assistant principal, district reading coordinator, director of curriculum and instruction, and curriculum consultant. She has extensive experience in reading, literacy, curriculum development, professional development, and continuous improvement processes.

Bob Noyed started his career as a newspaper reporter and freelance writer. Since then, he has worked in school communications and public relations at the state and national levels. He continues to write for both children and adult audiences. Bob lives in Woodbury, Minnesota.